"S T Kimbrough, Jr. has the unusual gift of taking words of ancient and medieval wisdom and rendering them into very contemporary verse. He even renders a few moderns like Ludwig Wittgenstein and St Teresa of Calcutta, and whoever thought they'd end up next to each other? This is deeply insightful wisdom. Keep it close at hand."

—TED A. CAMPBELL, professor of Wesley studies and church history,
Perkins School of Theology, Southern Methodist University

"These poetic paraphrases illuminate and sometimes expand upon ancient wisdom with insight, perspicacity, and often with great charm."

—PETER BOUTENEFF, founding director, Institute of Sacred Arts,
St. Vladimir's Orthodox Theological Seminary

"In some ways the chronological arrangement according to the dates of those quoted reminds me of Erasmus's *Adagia* and other Renaissance collections of wise sayings, except that instead of prose mini-essays, S T Kimbrough, Jr. has given his readers poetry. With careful consideration of the meters and rhyme schemes most appropriate for each saying, he turns ancient epigrams into meditations."

—JOHN H. ERICKSON, professor emeritus of church history,
St. Vladimir's Orthodox Theological Seminary

Ancient Wisdom
in Modern Verse

Ancient Wisdom in Modern Verse

Based on Texts from Greek and Latin Poets, Philosophers, Playwrights, Historians, and Apostolic and Early Church Fathers/Mothers

S T KIMBROUGH, JR.

Foreword by JOHN ERICKSON

RESOURCE *Publications* · Eugene, Oregon

ANCIENT WISDOM IN MODERN VERSE
Based on Texts from Greek and Latin Poets, Philosophers, Playwrights,
Historians, and Apostolic and Early Church Fathers/Mothers

Resource Publications
An Imprint of Wipf and Stock Publishers
199 W. 8th Ave., Suite 3
Eugene, OR 97401

www.wipfandstock.com

PAPERBACK ISBN: 978-1-6667-8544-9
HARDCOVER ISBN: 978-1-6667-8545-6
EBOOK ISBN: 978-1-6667-8546-3

Contents

CONTENTS

Section 2: From the Beginning of the Christian Era: Apostolic Fathers and Others

Section 3: Early Church Fathers/Mothers

Section 4: Post Eleventh Century to the Modern Era

CONTENTS

Foreword

When I was growing up in the Midwest many decades ago, I was awash in a sea of wisdom. Proverbs, maxims, truisms, sing-song rhymes, riddles, and old sayings were everywhere. They could be found in visual form on everything from advertisements and greeting cards to carefully crafted pieces of stitchery. They were on the lips of townsfolk and country farmers, of young and old. "Haste makes waste," our elders would tell us when we tried to race through our chores or homework. And occasionally there were also adaptations and parodies that attempted to render old maxims topical once more. "Do unto others before they do unto you—and then scram!" I am sure that other readers of S T Kimbrough's new book of verse can offer additional examples of the uses and abuses of popular wisdom.

Many of the words of wisdom that I remember best were scriptural or accepted as such, even when they were detached from their context or even manifestly non-scriptural. In a church service, the words "It is more blessed to give than to receive" (Acts 20:35) were a signal that a collection was about to be taken up. The oft-repeated motto "God helps those who help themselves" certainly is not scriptural, notwithstanding claims to the contrary among those who believe that self-reliant entrepreneurial types deserve success. It can be traced back to the fables of Aesop (6th century BCE) if not earlier. It first appears in English in the works of political theorist Algernon Sidney (1623–1683) and thereafter in Benjamin Franklin's *Poor Richard's Almanac*. This certainly isn't the message of Hebrew and Christian scripture. That is quite the opposite. God helps those who *cannot* help themselves. God is the helper of the helpless.

But sometimes even the most overused of old mottos and maxims and sayings can be welcome. I recall the wake for the wife of a normally taciturn neighbor, her husband for over sixty years. "Here today, gone tomorrow" was his most frequent response to friends who offered him their sympathy. The first recorded instance of this idiom occurs in an early English translation of John Calvin's *Life and Conversion of a Christian Man* (1549), where it was already referred to as proverbial. Neither my neighbor's words nor those of his friends were noteworthy for their originality. Rather, they illustrate how simple words of wisdom can help us negotiate the delicate rituals of bereavement and condolence. No matter how exalted, true wisdom has this-worldly implications and a wide range of practical applications, especially at life's most difficult moments.

In college and graduate school my interest in wisdom expanded in two directions, one academic, one religious. My major field of study was Renaissance and Reformation history and literature, where I concentrated on the contribution of humanists of the period to biblical studies and the publication of early Christian texts, Greek as well as Latin. Foremost among these humanist scholars was Desiderius Erasmus (1466–1536). Ecclesiastical historians remember him chiefly for his unsuccessful efforts to promote peace in a rapidly fracturing church. Cultural historians remember him also for his impact on literary forms and style. In his *Adagia* he gathered nuggets of ancient wit and wisdom and supplemented these with his own learned and elegant commentaries. By its final edition in 1536, *Adagia* entries numbered over four thousand. Their influence can still be felt in the modern essay.

My religious interest in wisdom springs from a different but related source: the liturgical worship and ethos of the Orthodox Church. This worship is wonderfully tangible, accessible, and inclusive. Its appeal is multi-sensory. It involves sight, sound, smell, touch, taste—something important with the erosion of printed book culture in our post-modern world. It tries to make the meaning of the incarnation readily accessible to everyone, including children and others who might otherwise be marginalized. It says to each and every one that the Transcendent One is near, that the Holy One wants us to participate in his holiness, that the Immortal One invites us to share in his eternal life.

Noteworthy is the role of the deacon (or in his absence the priest) at certain moments during Orthodox church services. "Wisdom! Let us arise!" and/or "Wisdom! Let us be attentive!" These are his commands at the clergy's initial entrance with the gospel book, before the epistle and gospel readings, and at other particularly wisdom-filled moments in the Divine Liturgy (the usual Orthodox term for the eucharistic service). At Vespers on certain occasions, readings taken most often from the sapiential and prophetic books of the Old Testament are introduced in much the same way. Throughout the scriptures, wisdom resounds. Its multiple expressions—whether in exhortation, admonition, consolation, prophecy, or good counsel—are celebrated. We are encouraged to go beyond the texts, not just to what lies behind them, in their historical context, but also to what lies before them, in the mystery of Christ, in our own lives and in the age to come.

The resounding voice of the classic Russian Orthodox deacon always reminds me of S T Kimbrough, magnificent singer, expert on hymnody, and author of the present volume, *Ancient Wisdom in Modern Verse*. He knows that the Orthodox tradition, like the Wesleyan, has a love of church singing, which is evident in its spirituality, its understanding of Scripture, and even in its ecclesiology—subjects that we explored together in a series of conferences in the early 2000s. I remember telling him at the time that with his voice he would make a terrific Orthodox deacon. He did not follow up on my suggestion.

The words of wisdom that S T has gathered in this volume come from many sources. Most—as his subtitle suggests—are "based on texts from Greek and Latin poets, philosophers, playwrights, historians, and early church fathers." These are grouped roughly chronologically from before the Christian era (16 entries), through the beginnings of the Christian era (16 entries), the early Fathers and Mothers of the Church (22 entries), into more recent times (9 entries). In some ways this arrangement reminds me of Erasmus's *Adagia* and other Renaissance collections of wise sayings, except that instead of prose mini-essays S T has given his readers poetry. With careful consideration of the meters and rhyme schemes most appropriate for each saying, he turns ancient epigrams into meditations.

Of these, S T's meditations on justice and social justice are his most passionate. With Sophocles, he asserts: "You shall not ration justice." That would be "the height of justice theft" (#4).[1] With Tertullian, he agrees that "you cannot parcel out freedom," for there is no such thing as "partial liberty" (#30). He cites the profound words of Basil the Great: "When someone steals another's clothes, we call him a thief. Should we not give the same name to one who could clothe the naked and does not?" (#38). More examples could be given. Concern for justice is essential for being truly human (#14), and an essential element of justice is concern for truth, especially at a time when "Alternative truth is in vogue / for those who truth would avoid" (#50).

Powerful also but in a quieter way are S T's meditations on the subject of silence and keeping silent. He agrees with Plato on the need to "engage the soul in quiet talk" (#12). He can say with Ignatius of Antioch, "It is better to be silent and be real than to talk and not be real" (#21); with Isidore of Pelusium, "To live without speaking is better than to speak without living" (#48); and with Abba Pambo and other desert dwellers that silence can edify more than speech (#24). It may even be, as John of the Cross tells us, that "silence is God's first language" (#60). But as a line from Euripides warns us, beware of the dangers of self-enslavement, when "You know the truth but hold your tongue, / you know the facts, say not a word" (#8).

1. The numbers within parentheses preceded by # are the numbers of the poems to which the author of the Foreword refers. The poems are numbered in sequence throughout the body of the book.

In "Hope Beyond Hatred," S T introduces his subject in an unusual way, with the words of an early Christian apologist, Justin Martyr. Justin defends Christians against the calumnies of their persecutors by lauding the way that they now live in harmony and fellowship with those whom they once hated. "These words of Justin Martyr"—S T observes—"both shame and fill us still with hope" (#23). Racial hatred and other ills still survive. But we still have hope. We dare to hope because, as Clement of Alexandria says, "If you do not hope, you will not find what is beyond your hopes" (#27). This is not just wishful thinking. We must look beyond the darkness of the present moment in confident expectation that the light of Christ will guide our steps. As the oft-repeated saying of Tertullian puts it, "Hope is patience with the lamp lit" (#29).

"Abide these three: faith, hope, and love, but the greatest of these is love," says St. Paul (I Corinthians 13:13). S T Kimbrough's poetry and his selection of quotations reflect this ordering of the cardinal virtues. Love—or charity, as the same Greek word, *agape*, often is translated – is preeminent because of its "simple truth" (#19). "It is love alone that gives worth to all things" (Teresa of Avila, #59). Without this, faith "does not actualize the light of spiritual knowledge in the soul" (Maximus the Confessor, #52). To be sure, there is a kind of love that burns out like a lamp that runs out of oil. But there is also "a love that is like a mighty spring gushing up out of the earth; it keeps flowing forever, and is inexhaustible" (Isaac of Nineveh, #54).

Most of the select words of wisdom in this collection are ancient, with very few later than the eleventh century, and almost none of the poems in the collection appear without a prefatory word. There is one noteworthy exception, S T's poem "On Being Human," a tribute to Mother Teresa of Calcutta and Albert Schweitzer, who "give us hope that love survives." As S T observes, "A human being's mystery / is filled with unique history" (#61). We finite human beings cannot expect to plumb this mystery or understand the complexities of this history. But recognizing our own finitude, may we in humility find the path to plenitude!

Fr. John Erickson
Peter N. Gramowich Professor of Church History Emeritus
and former Dean
St. Vladimir's Orthodox Theological Seminary
Yonkers, NY

Introduction

The wisdom of ancient savants, many of whom predate the Christian era, particularly historians, philosophers, poets, and playwrights of Greece, continues to be a source of insight into life well lived. The way in which the Greek tragedies address human conflict and the epitomes of knowledge, power, and love continues to reflect ongoing human ideals, turmoil, and emotion. However, for the public square today and social media options, they tend to be passé. Of course, there are still serious students of the Greek and Latin classics, and Syrian fathers of the Church who seem determined to keep these voices of the ancient past alive. This little book of poetry is an attempt to glean some of the gems of wisdom from them and from some of the Church Fathers/Mothers and to see their words and perspectives through the lens of contemporary life.

The *first section* of the book consists of reflections on sayings of philosophers, poets, historians, playwrights, and scientists of Greek and Latin traditions, who lived before the beginning of the Christian era: Pythagoras, Heraclitus, Aeschylus, Sophocles, Pericles, Euripides, Socrates, Plato, Aristotle, Cicero, and Virgil.

The *second section* consists of two parts. The first addresses sayings of the Apostolic Fathers. They are also known as the Ante-Nicene Fathers, who predate the Council of Nicaea in 325 AD, e.g., Clement 1 of Rome, Ignatius of Antioch, (St.) Barnabas, Justin Martyr, Theophilus of Antioch, and Origen. Three sages of this period who are not Apostolic Fathers but belong to this period of time are Josephus, Plutarch, and Marcus Aurelius.

The third section includes lyrical reflections on sayings of the Early Church Fathers, e.g., Cyprian, Athanasius of Alexandria, Basil the Great, Gregory of Nazianzus, Gregory of Nyssa, John Chrysostom, Augustine of Hippo, Amma Theodora, Maximus the Confessor, and Isaac of Nineveh.

The fourth section, "Post Eleventh Century to the Modern Era," addresses sayings of sages of the Church who represent a transition to the modern era and include Symeon the New Theologian, Hildegard of Bingen, Catherine of Siena, Ignatius Loyola, Teresa of Avila, John of the Cross, Mother Teresa, and Albert Schweitzer. Quotations of many other saints of the Church from the East and West could appear here as well, but the selections chosen for discussion emphasize the relevance and importance of their wisdom for the modern era.

At times I may reach past what the authors originally had in mind or I may miss an essential kernel of their thought, but I try not to make them say something foreign to their thinking. In our sophistication about the progress of knowledge, it is important to keep in mind that often the simplest assertions by scientists, linguists, historians, poets, playwrights, philosophers, and theologians of the distant past capture superbly many seminal ideas of what constitutes human pitfalls, but yet those aspects of human character and purpose that still make life meaningful.

The thinkers addressed here appear in chronological order by years of birth and death. This is not to suggest, however, that a chronological growth of knowledge is indicated. While early Greek savants are addressed first, they are followed by a significant number of the Apostolic and Post-Apostolic Fathers/Mothers, who play a significant role in crystalizing the primary doctrines of the church. There are perhaps more references here to the Post Apostolic Fathers/Mothers since I have read and studied them more closely over the years: Justin Martyr, Irenaeus of Lyons, Clement of Alexandria, and Origen. From the so-called "Golden Age" of Christianity (4th to 8th centuries) we read comments from Basil (bishop of Caesarea), Gregory (bishop of Nazianzus), Gregory (bishop of Nyssa), Isidore (bishop of Pelusium), and Maximus the Confessor. From the Latin Fathers of the same period there are selections from Tertullian, John Chrysostom, Augustine (bishop of Hippo), and from the Syriac Fathers Ephrem the Syrian and Isaac (bishop of Nineveh). From the Desert Fathers and Mothers there are excerpts from Symeon, the New Theologian, and Amma Theodora.

These traditions of wisdom and knowledge find comparable roots also in the wisdom literature of the Hebrew Scriptures and core writings from the intertestamental period. These traditions of wisdom are integral to the living of the Christian faith and extend into the modern period with thoughts from Catherine of Siena, Ignatius Loyola, Teresa of Avila, John of the Cross, Mother Teresa, and Albert Schweitzer. This is, however, just a taste of the ongoing importance of wisdom in the daily life of the Christian.

There is a certain practicality in almost all of the gems of wisdom quoted here immediately prior to the lyrical paraphrases, for these individuals of the ancient past sought to understand daily life in the context of sensible and ethical living. Each day was a new opportunity to perfect one's knowledge of the universe and the social context in which one is found. The Church Fathers have a Christological focus and seek to understand knowledge and its ethical practice through Christ's vision of daily living that involves the giving of self for others and God. They often use the simplest of metaphors, such as a beehive, to explain the axioms of faith and truth they address.

Emphasizing how the exploration of knowledge continues today to be integral to life's meaning and the journey of faith, two very different poems conclude the volume, stressing how the quest continues with such writers as Joyce, Becket, Wolff, Lawrence, and Faulkner. It continues as well in Picasso's abstract art, Schönberg's twelve-tone music, and other art forms, certainly worthy of further study. For those who ask whether there may be movement toward a synthesis of any kind, I ask what Wittgenstein and Lessing may have to offer.

Yes, there are many advances in the arenas of knowledge, many ways that aid us in enhancing knowledge: diverse analytical theories, the Internet, social media platforms, etc. And now with the development of Artificial Intelligence, one wonders if it is not particularly important to recover ancient gems of wisdom lest they become everyday comments supposedly placed in the mouths of modern human beings or as issuing from their pens and computers.

The author humbly submits these poetic paraphrases of ancient wisdom with the hope that they are faithful to these servants of wisdom, knowledge, and faith, and that they will capture the hearts, minds, and spirits of people today, for they have great value to enhance life's meaning.

S T Kimbrough, Jr.

SECTION 1

Before the Christian Era:
Greek and Latin philosophers, historians,
playwrights, poets, historians

PYTHAGORAS,[1] c. 570–c. 495

"Do not say a little in many words, but a great deal in a few."

1. Say More—Say Less

With words profuse to say little
   is talent indeed of many.
With every jot and tittle
   they're blessed, much blessed with a-plenty.

The gift of word economy
   that's found among a very few,
indeed is an anomaly
   a gift that more folk should accrue.

Economy of words says much
   that many words cannot express.
And many words are but a crutch,
   for you'll say more when you say less.

---

1. Pythagoras was a pre-Socratic, Ionian Greek philosopher from the island of Samos. His political and religious teachings influenced the philosophers Plato and Aristotle. Pythagoreanism emerged in the 6th century BCE based on the teachings and beliefs advanced by Pythagoras and his followers with a strong emphasis on communal life as illustrated in the first such community formed in the Greek colony of Kroton, which is modern Calabria in Italy.

HERACLITUS,[2] c. 540–480 BCE

"There is nothing permanent but change."

2. If Change, as Claimed, Is Permanent

If change, as claimed, is permanent,
    how permanent is change?
Some changes will be turbulent,
    while others will be strange.

If change alone is permanent,
    will we then accept change?
For some change is an ornament
    that others rearrange.

Some say a change is permanent,
    aver there's no more change,
and claim that they determine it—
    more change is out of range.

Yes, change is inevitable,
    that means that it exists.
But is it irrevocable,
    though surely change persists?

2. Heraclitus, also spelled Heraclietus, was a pre-Socratic, ancient Greek philosopher from Ephesus, who is known for his cosmology in which fire is considered essential to an orderly universe. Only fragments of one of his works remain.

AESCHYLUS,[3] c. 525/524–c. 456/455

"Memory is the mother of wisdom."

3. Mother of Wisdom

If wisdom's mother's memory
remembering all that may be,
a system of our body, mind
in which our thoughts are intertwined,
with memory we live and learn.
With memory we mark each turn,
each turn our lives may daily take,
the right or wrong turn that we make.
Our memory is a life force,
our memory keeps us on course.
So nurture memory each day
or memory's sure to decay!

---

3. Aeschylus is known as the father of Greek tragedy. Though he wrote some ninety plays, extant copies of only seven remain. He was one of the first playwrights to write in trilogy, e.g., *Orestes*.

SOPHOCLES,[4] c. 496–406 BCE

"If we are to keep our democracy, there must be one commandment:
You shall not ration justice."

4. Ration Justice?

To ration means there's scarcity
    of justice to be shared,
which creates much adversity,
    for justice is impaired.

To ration justice means the fall
    of our democracy.
there must, must be justice for all,
    not gross hypocrisy.

Just ration justice from the start,
    injustice then will reign,
and we with honesty will part,
    for justice is in vain.

One cannot say, "No rations left,"
    and say, "There's justice still."
This is the height of justice theft,
    and robs the people's will.

Do we still hear the people's cry,
    "Justice, justice for all"?
To ration justice will defy
    its worth once and for all.

---

4. With Euripides and Aeschylus, Sophocles was one of the great tragic
playwrights of Greece.

SOPHOCLES, c. 496–406 BCE

"A lie never lives to be old."

5. A Lie Never Lives to Be Old

A lie never lives to be old
by wise Sophocles we are told.

A lie may have life for a time,
adherents when it's in its prime.

Why is it that lies don't grow old?
because of a strong stranglehold!

A stranglehold of truth on lies,
the reason why lie on lie dies.

Though truth gives reason to persist,
a lie cannot with truth exist.

When facing truth, lies can't survive;
that's why lies cannot stay alive.

PERICLES,[5] c. 495 – 429 BCE

"Wait for the wisest of all counselors, time."

6. Wait for Time

We aren't wise if we wait and wait
    without wise counsel of time.
We wait for love, success, but fate
    has neither reason nor rhyme.

How can we learn, "wait patiently,"
    as time counsels us to do?
And why ignore time blatantly,
    as if fate has ignored you.

Time's counsel you'll find indeed wise.
    Time's counsel is worth the wait.
Time's counsel is full of surprise,
    Time's counsel may defy fate.

So let time wisely counsel you.
    Let time your wise couns'lor be.
Time's counsel, friend, never eschew.
    Time's counsel can set you free!

5. Pericles was an important Athenian statesman under whose leadership Athenian democracy thrived, with Athens becoming the cultural, religious, political, and economic center of Greece.

EURIPIDES,[6] c. 480–406 BCE

"Silence is true wisdom's best reply."

7. Silence

Is silence mere absence of speech,
when words do not create a breach?

Is silence mere choice to be mute,
refusal with words to dispute?

In silence the mind can be still;
in quiet one's thoughts can distill.

In stillness one can meditate:
new thoughts are born, new thoughts gestate.

Is silence wisdom's best reply?
Be silent! You'll discover why!

---

6. Euripides was an Athenian tragic poet/playwright. With Sophocles and Aeschylus, he was one of the great authors of Greek tragedy. Many of his plays are still extant. Particularly well known are *Medea*, *Electra*, and *The Trojan War*.

EURIPIDES, c. 480–406 BCE

"This is slavery, not to speak one's thoughts."

8. Self-Enslavement

What if you choose to self-enslave
    and do not dare to speak your thoughts?
Is this a strange way to behave,
    or common, feeble, out of sorts?

You know the truth but hold your tongue,
    You know the facts, say not a word.
Your silence leaves a jury hung,
    your silence leaves the truth all blurred.

If you refuse to speak your thoughts,
    a self-imposed, self-slavery,
your thinking may be tied in knots
    and make you seem unsavory.

HERODOTUS,[7] c. 484–c. 425 BCE

"I don't need a friend who changes when I change and who nods when I nod; my shadow does it much better."

9. My Shadow

A friend who changes when I change
    or nods when I would nod,
though it may seem to you quite strange,
    yet it's not strange, it's odd.

My shadow's better than my friend
    who nods with every smile,
whose changes never seem to end
    and does it with such style.

7. Herodotus was a Greek historian and geographer and is known particularly for his historical accounts of the Greco-Persian Wars.

SOCRATES,[8] c. 470–399 BCE

"Life without inquiry is not worth living."

10. Life Without Inquiry

No inquiry, can life have worth?
No inquiry, can thoughts have birth?
To live life fully ask and ask,
a quest for knowledge, lifelong task.
The more we ask, the more we learn,
the more our minds toward knowledge turn.
Enriched with knowledge we can live
much fuller lives with much to give.

8. Socrates was a distinguished Greek philosopher from Athens who is often known as the founder of Western philosophy and one of the first moral philosophers of the ethical tradition.

PLATO,[9] 428/7 or 424/423–348/7 BCE

"I am the wisest man alive. I know one thing, and that is that I know nothing."

11. The Wisest of All

Claim to know nothing, you're wise.
Could this be wisdom's high prize?

Ev'n Plato claimed it is so;
know nothing, you're in the know.

Thus, you're the wisest of all,
whose claim "the wise" will appall.

This claim invites one to learn,
for knowledge, wisdom to yearn.

9. Born in Athens, Plato was an ancient Greek philosopher who founded the Academy, a philosophical school where he taught philosophical ideas that would become known as Platonism.

PLATO, 428/7 or 424/3–348/347 BCE

"Thinking—the talking of the soul with itself."

12. Talking with the Soul

To think means converse with the soul,
    but how does this occur?
Who has this kind of self-control
    with one's soul to confer?

In silent moments the soul dares
    to stimulate our thought,
to waken often unknown cares
    till by them we are taught.

Engage the soul in quiet talk,
    fear not when it's awake.
A wakened soul will never balk
    when thinking is at stake.

ARISTOTLE,[10] 384-322 BCE

"At his best man is the noblest of all animals, separated from law and justice he is the worst."

13. Noblest of Animals?

Of animals upon the earth,
    which one's noblest of all?—
All human beings from their birth,
    yet they have one pitfall.

When they deny justice and law,
    they then become the worst,
like Jacob who betrayed Esau:
    his selfishness came first.

---

10. Aristotle was an ancient Greek philosopher and scientist who wrote on a plethora of subjects: e.g., physics, biology, zoology, logic, ethics, aesthetics, poetry, drama, music, economics, politics, and government.

MENANDER,[11] c. 342–292 BCE

"To refrain from all injustice renders us humane."

14. What Makes Someone Humane?

What makes someone humane?
One's born, is that not plain?
Humane's not who we are,
not who we are by far.
Humane you don't just get
as though it were a debt,
that destiny owes you
just because you're you.

Humane each one must learn,
humane one must discern.
Humane respects one's rights,
takes justice to new heights:
injustices decries,
injustices denies.
Humane we're one and all:
when injustices fall.

---

11. Menander was an Athenian dramatist and master of Greek New Comedy and wrote over 100 plays, a few of which survive: *Dyscolus* ("The Grouch"), *Epitrepontes* ("The Arbitration"), and *Samia* ("The Girl from Same").

CICERO,[12] 106–43 BCE

"A garden and a library are everything you need."

15. "A Garden and a Library"

"A garden and a library
   are everything you need,"
claimed Cicero's philosophy
   which we for wisdom read.

A garden and a library
   without care will not grow.
Love, nurture both are primary
   or we will little know.

A garden and a library
   were not all he would need.
He lacked the practicality
   to outlive Roman greed.[13]

12. Marcus Tullius Cicero was a Roman statesman, lawyer, scholar, philosopher.

13. Cicero was beheaded at the behest of Marc Anthony.

VIRGIL,[14] 70–19 BCE

16. From Mantua Young Virgil Came

From Mantua young Virgil came,
his destiny, a poet's fame.
A young Italian prodigy,
his work was an epiphany!

The *Aeneid* was his apogee,
the story of a refugee.
The refugee, Aeneas by name,
enjoyed also distinction, fame.

When Greeks took Troy, Aeneas fled.
His wanderings are the story thread
that Virgil weaves through many years
of Aeneas' travels, joys, and fears.

As if his lyrics wore a crown,
to Virgil came worldwide renown.
In Dante's *Divine Comedy*,
an echo of the *Odyssey*,

this Latin poet there is found;
the part he plays, deep and profound.
Each time you Dante's story tell,
it's Virgil leads the way through hell.

---

14. Publius Vergilius Maro was an ancient Latin-language Roman poet of the Augustan period, known as Virgil or Vergil. He wrote three of the most famous poems in Latin literature: the *Eclogues* (or *Bucolics*), the *Georgics*, and the *Aeneid*.

SECTION 2

From the Beginning of the Christian Era:
Apostolic Fathers and Others

JESUS,[15] 4 BCE–30/33 AD

"Blessed are the meek, for they will inherit the earth." (Matthew 5:5)

17. Blessed Are the Meek

The world awaits fulfillment still
    of Jesus' Sermon on the Mount.
Are meek the ones who suffer ill,
    with lives that often little count?

Who are the meek? The humble ones,
    who're easily imposed upon?
Are they submissive daughters, sons
    whose human rights are taken, gone?

A meek demeanor's often praised.
    Was this what Jesus had in mind?
Or is a larger question raised
    to which the proud are often blind?

The question of inheritance
    is prominent in Jesus' phrase,
but where then is the evidence
    the meek inherit earth always?

"Inherit the earth," Jesus said;
    Can this mean that the meek have rights
to earthly space before they're dead?
    This would take sharing to new heights.

15. Jesus was a first-century Jewish preacher and religious leader who is proclaimed in the Greek Scriptures as the Messiah and Savior of humankind.

ST. BARNABAS,[16] b. ? -c. 60 AD

"Family is the only real wealth."

18. Real Wealth

What misdirected wealth we seek:
    gold, silver, houses, money, lands.
Some people cannot last a week
    without possessions in their hands.

We learn of diamonds' extreme worth
    and other precious, valued stones.
Yet all when they depart this earth,
    have nothing but their skin and bones.

St. Barnabas gives us a clue
    where wealth that's real indeed may lie.
It's not found in what we accrue,
    in things that we can quantify.

There's only one wealth that is real;
    St. Barnabas says, "family."
The wealth supreme that all may feel:
    reality is family.

The family of humankind
    is one to which we all belong.
A family for all to find:
    you've relatives your whole life long.

---

16. According to tradition Barnabas was an important early Christian disciple in Jerusalem. According to the Book of Acts he was a Cypriot Jew who was named an apostle (Acts 4:36; 14:14), and who had a close association with Paul the apostle. He was thought to be the author of the Epistle of Barnabas.

Speak to a neighbor, make a friend,
   a homeless mother, father, child.
All families have but one end:
   a mutual care that is love-styled.

POPE CLEMENT I,[17] c. 35 – c. 99

"Charity unites us to God. There is nothing mean in charity. Charity knows no schism, does not rebel, does all things in accord."

19. The Simple Truth of Charity

The simple truth of charity
   is—unity not schism.
The simple truth of charity
   is—it refutes racism.

The simple truth of charity
   is—it does not rebel.
The simple truth of charity
   is—it does all things well.

The simple truth of charity
   is—it does nothing mean.
The simple truth of charity:
   is—much from it to glean.

The simple truth of charity
   is—it unites to God.
The simple truth of charity
   is—some will find this odd.

17. Pope Clement I is also known as Clemens Romanus in Latin. Both Irenaeus and Tertullian refer to him as the bishop of Rome from 88 until his death in 99. He is known as the first of the Apostolic Fathers. Tertullian believed him to have been consecrated the fourth pope by St. Peter the Apostle. The *First Letter of Clement* (or the *Letter to the Church of Corinth*) is considered by many to be the most important first-century Christian document besides the New Testament. He has been credited with transmitting to the church the *Ordinances of the Holy Apostles Through Clement (Apostolic Constitutions).*

The simple truth of charity
    is—charity's divine.
The simple truth of charity
    is—it is yours and mine!

JOSEPHUS,[18] c. 37 – c. 100 AD and CICERO, 106–43 BCE

20. Josephus of Jerusalem

Josephus of Jerusalem
   and Cicero of Rome,
what values do we find in them
   with which to feel at home?

For Roman-Jewish history
   Josephus' clever pen
gives insight to antiquity:
   what happened where and when.

For rhetoric, philosophy,
   we turn to Cicero,
whose oratory thoughtfully
   is wisdom's *quid pro quo*.

From both we learn to reason, think,
   hence both we still must read;
we'll find these authors interlink.
   Yes, both of them we need.

18. Josephus was a first-century Roman-Jewish historian who was born in Jerusalem and is best known for his volume *The Jewish War*.

IGNATIUS OF ANTIOCH,[19] b. ? - c. 110

"It is better to be silent and be real than to talk and not be real."

21. How Can Silence Make us Real?

How can silence make us real?
Is this something we can feel?
Without speech can we be real?
Why does silence have appeal?
Always think before you speak
or your options are quite bleak.
Others will know you're not real,
for just words have no appeal.

When you're silent, you can think.
When you're silent, there's a link,
there's a link to thought process.
Silence needs this to address
all the things that matter most
for which silence is the host!
How can silence make you real?
Try it! You'll find its appeal!

---

19. Ignatius of Antioch, one of the Apostolic Fathers, was also known as Ignatius Theophorus, an early Christian author and bishop of Antioch. He is known particularly for seven letters written as a Roman prisoner in which he defended the authority of the New Testament and opposed the Docetists, who did not accept Christ's suffering and death as real.

PLUTARCH,[20] c. 46–119

"The measure of life is its beauty, not its length."

22. Life's Measure

If we ask, What is life's measure,
    how shall we then respond?
Will we answer what we treasure,
    state first of what we're fond?

Will it be good health, to be rich,
    to live a long, long time?
Or could it be we don't know which
    to emphasize as prime.

Of beauty do we ever think
    by which to measure life?
Perhaps it is a missing link
    with shapes and colors rife.

For beauty's richness fills each day
    and shares what matters most;
for beauty's richness holds in sway
    the peace, love often lost.

---

20. Plutarch was a Greek Platonist philosopher, historian, essayist, and priest at the Temple of Apollo in Delphi.

JUSTIN MARTYR,[21] 100–165

"We used to hate and destroy one another and refused to associate with people of another race or country. Now, because of Christ, we live together with such people and pray for our enemies."

23. Hope Beyond Hatred

These words of Justin Martyr
　　both shame and fill us still
with hope, or a non-starter,
　　for hate has its own will.

Would that "used to" were the truth,
　　but I fear it is not.
Destroy and hate from my youth
　　devised a dreadful plot.

Justin Martyr in his time
　　thought that because of Christ
that harmony was in its prime,
　　but it was sacrificed.

Racism's hatred still survives
　　though Christ came long ago.
Enmity has many lives
　　which Christians know is so.

Justin's words of hope we mourn,
　　but live to realize,
Christ our prejudice has borne,
　　in him enmity dies.

21. Also known as Justin the Philosopher, Justin was an early Christian apologist as revealed in his work the *First Apology*, in which he defends Christian morality and attempts to persuade the Roman emperor, Antonius, to desist from persecuting the Christian church. His *Second Apology* was addressed to the Roman Senate. There are other surviving works as well.

33

THEOPHILUS,[22] ARCHBISHOP OF ANTIOCH, c. 115–c. 183–185

Theophilus came to Scetis one day. The brethren who were assembled said to Abba Pambo, "Say something to the Archbishop, so that he may be edified." The old man said to them, "If he is not edified by my silence, he will not be edified by my speech."

24. Edification of Silence

Will those who're edified by speech,
    be edified by silence?
Is silence far beyond their reach,
    and do they know the diff'rence?

If silence does not edify,
    then what about constant speech?
Will non-stop utt'rance nullify
    whatever one's words might teach?

Let silence edify our thoughts,
    let silence shape what we say,
for constant speaking will cast lots
    till our thoughts are cast away.

22. Theophilus converted to Christianity as an adult and rose to be archbishop of Antioch. He is known best for his apologetic tracts *To Autolycus,* a non-believing friend who derided Christianity and thus prompted Theophilus' strong defense.

IRENAEUS OF LYONS,[23] 130–202

"The initial step for us all to come to the knowledge of God is the contemplation of nature."

25. The Knowledge of God

To come to the knowledge of God
    do I begin with holy writ,
or first by nature should be awed?
    Must I to one of these commit?

Irenaeus saw first the need
    of Scripture's strong authority:
a scriptural canon and a creed,
    yet he chose flexibility.

The first step's not to read the Word,
    to come to know of God divine.
No matter what you may have heard,
    this knowledge nature will refine.

---

23. Irenaeus of Lyons was a Greek bishop and leading theologian of the second century who advanced the authoritative canon of Scriptures, the creed, and the authority of the episcopal office.

MARCUS AURELIUS,[24] 121–180

"If it's not right, don't do it, if it's not true, don't say it."

26. Lost Ancient Wisdom

This ancient wisdom now is lost,
is lost at a tremendous cost!
Have we lost knowledge of what's right?
Is moral judgment out of sight?
If it's not right, do it and lie;
stick by what's wrong until you die.
This is some politicians' creed:
Don't give a damn what others need!
Marcus Aurelius we lament—
Can we recover his intent?

24. Marcus Aurelius, who reigned as Roman emperor from 161 to 180 AD, was also a philosopher and the last ruler of the *Pax Romana*, i.e., the age of peace.

CLEMENT OF ALEXANDRIA,[25] c. 150–c. 215

"If you do not hope, you will not find what is beyond your hopes."

27. Hope Beyond Hope

Is hope somehow in each of us,
    though it may dormant lie?
Is hope a word some won't discuss,
    ev'n when they don't know why?

The hope that has a single goal
    one cannot look beyond,
yet without hope one robs the soul
    of will to fight, go on.

If you decide to hope, take care
    that it's no dead-end street.
No hope beyond your hope's a snare
    where hopelessness you'll greet.

25. His original name was Titus Flavius Clemens, a Christian theologian and philosopher who taught at the Catechetical School of Alexandria and was the mentor of Origen and Alexander of Jerusalem.

CLEMENT OF ALEXANDRIA, c. 150–c. 215

*"When lies have been accepted for some time, the truth always as-
tounds with an air of novelty."*

28. Truth Is Truth

When one accepts lies for some time,
   the truth seems quite a novelty.
Though some lies are indeed a crime;
   some lies are subtle cruelty.

Some lies intend to do no harm;
   they stretch the truth to an extreme,
and trust that they will cause no harm;
   they smile and further some bad scheme.

The truth is truth the facts bear out;
   to smother it will lead astray.
The truth is truth and leaves no doubt,
   but lies will always truth betray!

But there are truths borne in the heart,
   eternal truth born not of lies:
the truth of love's eternal art,
   and truth divine to save the wise.

TERTULLIAN,[26] c. 155–c. 220

"Hope is patience with the lamp lit."

29. Hope

"Hope is patience with the lamp lit."
    It needs not await the light,
for it with light is closely knit
    and lights the way through the night.

Through patience hope's lamp burns and burns,
    no matter where you may go.
No matter if one yearns and yearns
    hope's lamp does not lose its glow.

The light of hope's lamp you may hide,
    and think its flame you've put out.
The light of hope's lamp will abide,
    survives ev'n the strongest doubt.

To follow with patience the light
    is not the simplest of things.
But if you but keep it in sight,
    you'll find that your spirit sings.

---

26. Tertullian, whose Latin name was Quintus Septimius Florens Tertullianus, was from Carthage. He produced an extensive Christian literature in Latin. As an early Christian apologist, he opposed heresies such as Christian Gnosticism. Tertullian is sometimes called the father of Latin Christianity and the founder of Western theology.

TERTULLIAN, c. 155–c. 220

"You cannot parcel out freedom in pieces because freedom is all or nothing."

30. Parceling Out Freedom

Defining freedom's been a game
    for centuries on end,
that's played by rulers one can name,
    who all for pow'r contend.

The Pharaohs of great Egypt land
    whose pyramids slaves built,
or Chinese dynasties that banned
    all foreigners without guilt.

Or Jewish years of jubilee
    when some slaves could go free,
left others without choice to be
    enslaved, yes legally.

There is no partial liberty
    though humans make it so.
It is the greatest travesty:
    "a few we will let go."

For freedom to be parceled out
    as if one had this right,
is unjust and without a doubt,
    a ghastly human blight.

ORIGEN OF ALEXANDRIA,[27] c. 185–c. 253

"The power of choosing good and evil is within the reach of all."

31. Within the Reach of All

The pow'r to choose evil or good:
we do or don't do as we should.
All have this mighty pow'r to choose:
the pow'r by which each one may lose,
or pow'r by which good may attain
the chance to make humans humane.
This pow'r of choice is within reach
of all, who by choice others teach
to cast out evil, promote good,
from childhood until adulthood.

27. He is also known as Origen Adamantius, an early Christian scholar and theologian who spent the first part of his career in Alexandria. A prolific writer, he produced over 2,000 treatises on diverse aspects of theology, biblical exegesis, homiletics, and textual criticism.

ORIGEN OF ALEXANDRIA, c. 185–c. 253

"Conscience is the chamber of justice."

32. Conscience, the Chamber of Justice

In us there's a justice chamber
　　whenever conscience is allowed.
It's there so we can remember
　　that truth must always be avowed.

Without conscience there's no justice.
　　Without conscience truth surely dies.
Without conscience no one trusts us.
　　Without conscience there are but lies.

Yes, justice thrives where there's conscience,
　　when conscience truth does not forget.
We lose justice in its absence,
　　for justice remains in its debt!

SECTION 3

Early Church Fathers/Mothers

CYPRIAN,[28] c. 210–258

"Think not that you are thus maintaining the Gospel of Christ when you separate yourself from the flock of Christ."

33. Maintaining the Gospel?

How has the Gospel been maintained
    by constant church divisions?
How has the Gospel been sustained
    by constant church collisions?

To love, we read, the Gospel's goal
    and love one's enemies too,
for "God is love," this is the soul
    of what Christ's followers do.

How senseless Christians make this claim,
    for they themselves don't agree.
Love those who think like you, their aim,
    this love can set no one free.

We cannot count the divisions
    of the separated flock,
for there are countless revisions
    that claim that they are the rock,

the rock on which Christ built the church,
    the foundation that is true.
Yet new divisions will besmirch
    the Gospel love as untrue.

---

28. Cyprian was bishop of Carthage and an early Christian writer of Berber descent and pre-eminent writer of Latin works.

ATHANASIUS OF ALEXANDRIA,[29]
c. 296 or 298–373

"You cannot put straight in others what is warped in yourself."

34. How Easily, Often We Try

How easily, often we try
　　to change that which is wrong.
We're sure we see with keenest eye
　　where wrong does not belong.

In others it is plain to see
　　where change is needed first.
It is so clear, decidedly,
　　as I with counsel burst.

But then quite unexpectedly
　　a friend plainly points out:
"The flaw in someone else you see
　　is yours without a doubt."

Be careful lest the flaw you see
　　in others is your own.
Think not they need your charity
　　until your own has flown.

29. He is also known as Athanasius the Great, Athanasius the Confessor, and among Coptic Christians he bears the name Athanasius the Apostolic. He was the twentieth pope of Alexandria, with a tenure spanning forty-five years. He was the first apologetic Orthodox theologian to write in Coptic and Greek, and many of his polemical writings defending against pagan beliefs and practices constituted some of the first works to shape core ideas of Orthodox theology. See *Orations Against the Arians, Against the Heathen, The Incarnation of the Word of God*; also, *On the Incarnation, On the Holy Spirit,* and many more.

EPHREM THE SYRIAN,[30] 306–373

"No one is truly poor except the one who lacks the truth."

35. The Truly Poor

Ephrem the Syrian says the poor
    are those who simply lack the truth,
in every instance truth immure
    perhaps by lying from their youth.

Many well-dressed, fashion prone
    are poor but do not look the part.
In every sinew, every bone
    they are impoverished from the start.

You're poor if truth indeed you lack.
    You're poor if truth you don't regard.
You're poor if truth you would attack
    and hoist lies on your own petard.

30. He is also known as Saint Ephrem, Ephrem of Edessa or Aprem of Nisibis, and he is known as one of the most important early Christian hymnographers as revealed in his numerous poetic renderings of Scripture and theology.

BASIL THE GREAT,[31] 330–379

"Plant kindness and you'll gather love."

36. Plant kindness and You'll gather love.

Plant kindness and you'll gather love,
a plan that no one is above.
Just read Leviticus[32] again
where love of neighbor's very plain.

At times one's kindness seems in vain,
but kindness shared, returns again.
At times the kindness shared seems lost,
but kindness surely's worth the cost.

Results so often we can't see,
the signs, effects of charity.
That is no reason not to share,
for many people need our care.

31. Basil the Great was an early church father and bishop of Caesarea, who defended the Orthodox faith against the Arian heresy and supported the Nicene Creed. He wrote important works on monasticism, theology, and canon law. Basil also had a keen ability to balance theological convictions and political connections of his time.

32. Lev. 19:18, "Love your neighbor as yourself."

BASIL THE GREAT, 330–379

"Whoever sows courtesy reaps friendship, and whoever plants kindness gathers love."

37. The Daily Sower

Are you aware each day you plant
    some seeds that grow and grow?
The harvest you may think is scant,
    but you will find, not so.

Sow courtesy and reap a friend;
    sow anger, anger reap.
Sow kindness, reap love without end.
    This harvest you may keep.

BASIL THE GREAT, 330–379

*"When someone steals another's clothes, that person is called a thief.
Should not the same name be given to one who could clothe the naked
and does not? The bread in your cupboard belongs to the hungry, the
coat unused in your closet belongs to the one who needs it; the shoes
rotting in your closet belong to the one who has no shoes; the money
which you hoard up belongs to the poor."*

38. It's Mine

"It's mine," often we're prone to say.
"It's mine," because I always pay.
I pay the price to make it mine;
I pay the price "mine" to define.
So what! My cupboard's very full
with clothing, food, a basketful.
Come hard times, I will need it all,
so I won't suffer, stumble, fall.
Give some to others who are poor?
How foolish that would be, for sure.
If I have food and you have not,
why should I share what I have got?
How true the news "nothing you own"—
a moment's here, and then it's flown.
Are you a thief if you don't share?
St. Basil makes us all aware:
indeed we're robbing from the poor.
If we make certain we're secure,
secure within our cupboards there
and only with ourselves will share.
Someone is cold and needs a coat,
that I have two, sit up, take note.
If you work hard, earn your own keep,
you'll find a coat that's very cheap.

Yes, thieves we are without a doubt,
we're thieves who will help no one out!

GREGORY OF NAZIANZUS,[33] 329–390

"We are not made for ourselves alone, we are made for the good of all our fellow creatures."

39. We Are Not Made for Self Alone

We are not made for self alone,
an idea sometimes we own,
a thought sometimes that we condone.
We're made for fellow creatures' good,
but do we think we really should
be this concerned from our childhood?

For fellow creatures be concerned,
concerned for what they've never earned,
ev'n when our friendship they have spurned,
for when we for the others care,
the others know the other's there,
quite ready of oneself to share.

33. A fourth-century Archbishop of Constantinople, he is also known as Gregory the Theologian, and is known as one of the foremost theologians in the history of Greek Christianity. His contributions to the field of pneumatology, the theology concerning the nature of the Holy Spirit, are particularly significant.

GREGORY OF NAZIANZUS, 329–390

"For nothing is so pleasant to men as talking of other people's business, especially under the influence of affection or hatred, which often almost entirely blinds us to truth."

40. How Pleasant, How Pleasant to Men

How pleasant, how pleasant to men,
again and again and again,
another's business to discuss
and make a most unneeded fuss.
Another's business leave alone,
for you will only make them groan.
You praise them, you'll find they are glad,
You criticize them, they'll be sad.
To truth you are so often blind,
since only your thoughts come to mind!

GREGORY OF NYSSA,[34] 335–395

"It is impossible to live without tears who considers things exactly as they are."

41. Things as They Are

To see things as they really are
    is cause for many tears.
The poor are poorer now by far
    than in the foregone years.

While wars bring people to their knees,
    intolerance and greed
produce a flood of refugees—
    without hope for their need.

A year-long drought that devastates
    a region and its farms,
brings hunger and death estimates
    from starvation alarms.

At times it seems that nature's force
    is also evil too,
its winds can shape a deadly course,
    destroying all in view.

Life without tears, unthinkable,
    each moment passes by
when evil seems invincible.
    We weep and we ask, why?

---

34. He is also known as Gregory of Nyssa and bishop of Nyssa in Cappadocia, who led the struggle against the Arians.

GREGORY OF NYSSA, 335–395

"The silent painting speaks on the walls and does much good."

42. A Silent Painting Speaks

A silent painting on the walls
    says nothing, yet it speaks.
A person's eye upon it falls
    and carefully it seeks.

It seeks the depths of wonders there
    that vary with each look.
One stands entranced, as if to stare,
    at each line and each nook.

The painting speaks in contoured lines,
    in colored springs and brooks.
It speaks through trails and rustling pines
    a speech not found in books.

The painter's speech is quite unique,
    in contemplation borne;
it shapes the images that speak—
    imagination's born.

JOHN CHRYSOSTOM,[35] 347–407

"A moth gnaws a garment as does envy consume a person."

43. Envy

Like moths that gnaw at a garment
   until there's nothing left.
If envy turns into torment,
   it leaves the soul bereft.

We're trapped by thoughts that don't expire,
   bereft of love and care
for those who have what we desire,
   if envy's always there.

By envy one may be consumed,
   consumed, fully devoured,
for envy strikes a mortal wound
   and one is overpowered.

35. John Chrysostom was an early Church Father known particularly for his biblical interpretation, eloquent preaching, and outreach to common people with concern for the spiritual and temporal needs of the disadvantaged.

JOHN CHRYSOSTOM, 347–407

*"The bee is more honored than other animals not because she labors,
but because she labors for others."*

44. Beehive Mentality

In all creation honey bees
    live lives that are unique.
Their goal is not themselves to please;
    it's common good they seek.

They labor not for self alone
    but for their colony.
In their activity there's shown
    beehive economy.

Each worker bee cares for the hive,
    brings pollen, nectar in,
the queens keep worker bees alive;
    through them all bees begin.

What if all humankind took cues
    from bees on how to live?
No one would daily tasks refuse,
    but each to each would give.

JOHN CHRYSOSTOM, 347–407

"A friend is more to be longed for than light; I speak of a genuine one. And wonder not, for it were better for us that the sun should be extinguished than that we should be deprived of friends, better to live in darkness, than to be without friends."

45. Life Without Friends?

It's "better to live in darkness
    than to be without friends,"
as if the heavens were starless,
    the moon no brightness lends.

Imagine our own galaxy—
    no stars, no moon, no sun,
and without light, what agony,
    no friends, no life, no fun.

Imagine living without friends,
    without a warm embrace,
without a word that kindness lends,
    of friendly love, no trace.

A friend brings light into our lives
    that helps us all to see,
that light through darkest times survives.
    True friends make darkness flee.

AUGUSTINE OF HIPPO,[36] 354–430

"Is anyone skillful enough to have fashioned himself?"

46. The Great Fashioner

We humans like to fashion
ourselves with a great passion:
become what we have not been,
become what we have not seen.
We think of self as most kind,
or someone with a keen mind.
Sometimes self-fashion is true,
sometimes self-fashion's askew.
Though fashion self as we may,
and learn new skills every day,
Bold Augustine's sure to ask:
Who's skilled enough for the task?—
The task of fashioning you,
creating the you that's you?

---

36. Augustine, a theologian and philosopher, was bishop of Hippo Regius in
Numidia, Roman North Africa.

AUGUSTINE OF HIPPO, 354–430

*"Whatever marvel happens in this world, it is certainly less marvelous
than this whole world itself."*

47. Marvelous Creation

Amazing things can still transpire,
one saves an infant from a fire.
A castle standing on the Rhine,
whose beauty, elegance combine,
combine with lovely forest slopes
that give the human spirit hopes.
How often wonders we await,
some extraordinary fate
of things unusual and strange
that our confused lives rearrange
in patterns of a new success
where less is more and more is less.
Why is it wonders we await
when we forget to concentrate
on wonders that creation brings,
quite often in the simplest things.
When doves in quiet incubate
two eggs until they both gestate,
and season wonders change by year,
just think of wonders that are here.
We need no miracle to know
that wonders in creation show
how wondrous and miraculous,
how charming and how fabulous
are nature's wonders to be seen,
a sunrise or a sunset scene.
We stand at every day's new start
and marvel that we are a part

of new creation taking place,
for each day nature makes a space
for all her wonders to be seen,
a miracle in every scene.

ISIDORE OF PELUSIUM,[37] b. ?–436

"To live without speaking is better than to speak without living. For the former who lives rightly does good even by his silence, but the latter does no good even when he speaks. When words and life correspond to one another they are together the whole of divine philosophy."

48. To Speak, to Live

For many to speak is to live
    for others to live is to speak,
but is there more than these to give?
    Of silence what then should we seek?

To live without speech is better,
    than to speak and never to live.
If one lives not by the letter,
    then silence has so much to give.

Yes, speech can mean mere spoken words,
    which space may fill and do no good.
They rumble like thunder of herds,
    and do no one good as they should.

If speaking and living are one
    and each complements the other,
divine philosophy has won,
    for they're then sister and brother.

37. Isidore was born in Egypt to an important Alexandrian family which included the Alexandrian Patriarchs Theophilus and Cyril. He was a student of secular disciplines but eventually withdrew for a time to desert solitude. He eventually returned to Pelusium, where he was ordained to the priesthood. After some years he retired to monastery life, where he wrote numerous epistles on diverse theological subjects, of which hundreds survive.

AMMA THEODORA,[38] 5TH CENTURY

"Neither asceticism, nor vigils, nor any kind of suffering are able to save.
Only true humility can do that."

49. Humility

Try what we may ourselves to save:
  self-discipline, reflection,
or suffering that the way might pave
  to our own self-protection.
Without humility no way,
  no path leads to salvation.
All other paths will lead astray,
  and only to vexation.

Stripped of conceit and selfish pride,
  and views of one's importance,
humility will be our guide
  to life of worth and substance.
Humilty indeed can save
  all humankind from downfall;
it transforms all that can deprave
  from dawn until the nightfall.

---

38. Theodora is one of the women known as the Desert Mothers (*amma* or
spiritual mother).

BENEDICT OF NURSIA,[39] 480–547

"There is nothing better to display the truth in an excellent light, than a clear and simple statement of facts."

50. Truth and Facts

If truth you clearly would display
   within an excellent light,
you will suspicions cast away
   by stating clearly what's right.

Alternative truth is in vogue
   for those who truth would avoid;
they play the role of spoiler, rogue
   when clear facts they declare void.

Alternative truth is a sham,
   has nothing to do with facts.
Alternative truth is a scam—
   results in dishonest acts.

If truth you clearly would display
   within an excellent light,
facts will suspicions drive away
   clear facts will falsehood indict!

39. Benedict was the founder of the Benedictine monastery at Monte Cassino and is known as the father of Western monasticism. He established the Benedictine Rule which became the basis of monastic living throughout much of Europe.

MAXIMUS THE CONFESSOR,[40] c. 580-662

"If life always went well, would we not become so attached to our present state, even though we know it will not last, and by deception become enslaved to pleasure? In the end we would think that our present life is the best and noblest, and forget that, being made in the image of God, we are destined for higher things."

51. Destined for Higher Things

If we think life always goes well,
    though we know it's not so,
deceived would we in pleasure dwell,
    none other seek to know?

Why should we hope for better times
    when we are satisfied?
The status quo with our heart rhymes;
    it's to the present tied.

But will we then forget the thought:
    in God's image we're made,
and higher things are to be sought?
    Thus destiny's not stayed!

---

40. Maximus the Confessor was a Byzantine theologian of the seventh century and a prolific writer of commentaries on the Greek Church Fathers, which greatly influenced the theology and mysticism of the Middle Ages.

MAXIMUS THE CONFESSOR, c. 580–662

"Just as the thought of fire does not warm the body, so faith without love does not actualize the light of spiritual knowledge in the soul."

52. Faith and Love

Only to think about a fire,
    will never keep your body warm.
No matter that you faith desire,
    without love, faith cannot take form.

Without love, faith cannot have light
    and will not benefit the soul,
no growth of spirit is in sight,
    for love it is that is faith's goal.

ISAAC OF NINEVEH,[41] c. 613-c. 700

"Make peace with yourself and both heaven and earth will make peace with you."

53. Make Peace with Yourself

Make peace with myself, I am told,
    but first must I see I'm at war?
The conflicts within both new and old
    I cannot, I cannot ignore.

To make peace with self's no small task,
    for I must my foibles admit,
be honestly willing to ask—
    What are they? Admit them and quit?

The first step to finding my peace:
    see heav'n and earth immense and vast,
and let my own self-pride decrease,
    for when I'm gone, they'll me outlast.

The humble self has the best chance
    to find peace in the universe,
the cause of earth's peace to advance.
    and others in peace to immerse.

---

41. He was also known as Saint Isaac the Syrian, Abba Isaac, Isaac Syrus, and Isaac of Qatar. He was a seventh-century Syriac Christian bishop and theologian, best known for his works on Christian asceticism.

ISAAC OF NINEVEH, c. 613–c. 700

"There is love like a small lamp, which goes out when the oil is consumed; or like a stream which dries up when it doesn't rain. But there is a love that is like a mighty spring gushing up out of the earth; it keeps flowing forever, and is inexhaustible."

54. What kind of Love Is Yours

What kind of love is yours,
a love that lasts, endures?

Like lamps that have no oil,
empty and are light's foil?

Are you of love devoid,
at all costs love avoid?

Does love from you gush forth
like rains from south or north?

Is your love like a spring,
artesian offering,

that lets your love flow on
from darkness till the dawn?

This is the love divine
that is yours and is mine.

SECTION 4

Post Eleventh Century to the Modern Era

SYMEON THE NEW THEOLOGIAN,[42] 949-1022

"If you know that all visible things are a shadow and all pass away, are you not ashamed of playing with shadows and hoarding transitory things? Like a child you draw water with a bucket full of holes; do you not realize it and take it into account, my dear friend? As though there were nothing more serious than appearance and illusion, as though reality has been taken from them."

55. All Things Pass Away

If all things truly pass away,
    why hoard transitory things?
Yes, life is simply made this way,
    all earthly things will take wings.

Like a child will you draw water
    with a bucket filled with holes?
Like a thoughtless son or daughter
    are you lacking all controls?

Appearance or an illusion,
    why not face reality?
You will come to the conclusion:
    it is sensibility!

42. St. Symeon was a poet and monk of Eastern Orthodoxy and one of the last three saints canonized by the Eastern Orthodox Church and given the title of "Theologian." The two others were John the Apostle and Gregory of Nazianzus.

HILDEGARD OF BINGEN,[43] c. 1098 – 1179

"Glance at the sun. See the moon and the stars. Gaze at the beauty of earth's greetings. Now, think. What delight God gives to humankind with all these things, All nature is at the disposal of humankind. We are to work with it, for without it we cannot survive." . . . *"All creation is a song of praise to God."*

56. Glance at the Sun, the Moon, the Stars

Glance at the sun, the moon, the stars,
the heavens on to planet Mars.
Gaze now beyond our galaxy
to sights Hildegard could not see.
Is this creation still a song
of praise to God for ages long?

How can the sights we cannot see
be praise to a divinity?
The mystery is mystery;
it's thus and will forever be!
What a responsibility
for human ingenuity.

Creation care for humankind
expands the vision of the mind.
We know not where creation ends,
responsibility it lends.
Creation is indeed alive,
work with creation to survive.

---

43. Known also as Saint Hildegard and the Sibyl of the Rhine, she was a German Benedictine abbess, writer, creation-centered mystic, philosopher, visionary, and composer of sacred monophony. She authored theological works, letters, and composed antiphons, hymns, and chants.

CATHERINE OF SIENA,[44] 1347–1383

"It is only through shadows that one comes to know the light."

57. Shadow and Light

A shadow's born when light is blocked
    and light cannot extend its rays.
and for the moment light is locked
    within itself, and there it stays.

As darkness takes the place of light,
    creating a foreboding scene;
the darkness will decrease your sight;
    you may not know where you have been.

But light can overcome the dark,
    for darkness cannot hide from light.
One's grateful for the slightest spark
    that can a flame of light ignite.

Bypass the shadows into light;
    seek always there to stay.
Life lived in light avoids the plight
    of light that is shadowed away.

44. Catherine was an Italian who became a member of the Third Order of Saint Dominic of the Roman Catholic Church. As a mystic and author, she is known for her treatises *The Dialogue of Divine Providence*. She was the second woman to be declared a "Doctor of the Church."

IGNATIUS OF LOYOLA,[45] 1491–1556

"Laugh and grow strong."

58. Ignatius on Laughter

Ignatius said, "Laugh and grow strong."
   Hence laughter is a healthy sign.
Does this mean not to laugh is wrong?
   No, laughter won't make health decline.

If anything, it gives you strength.
   With laughter you can face the worst,
endure the good and bad at length
   and be with laughter poised to burst.

With laughter you'll make sad folks smile.
   With laughter you'll make burdens light.
With laughter you'll downcast beguile.
   With laughter you'll make dark days bright.

---

45. Ignatius of Loyola was a Spanish Catholic priest and theologian, who has often been misquoted, and "laugh and grow strong" may indeed be such a misquotation; nevertheless it persists in connection with him. With Peter Faber and Francis Xavier, he founded the Society of Jesus (Jesuits).

TERESA OF AVILA,[46] 1515–1582

"It is love alone that gives worth to all things."

59. Love Alone

Yes, prized above prestige and health,
  one thing alone gives all things worth,
more valued than position, wealth,
  it's love in us that needs new birth.

Love will consumer standards change,
  for love gives, cares, and always shares.
Yes, love's economy is strange
  to worldly, selfish, greedy snares.

Alone love gives worth to all things;
  consumer standards though say, "No!
No! It's from worldly things worth springs!"
  But love responds, "Such worth forego!"

46. She is also known as Saint Teresa of Jesus, although her original name was Teresa de Cepeda y Ahumada, born in Avila, Spain. She is one of the distinguished mystics of Roman Catholicism, author of spiritual classics, and originator of the Carmelite Reform with its strong emphasis on contemplative life.

JOHN OF THE CROSS,[47] 1542–1591

"Silence is God's first language."

60. God's First Language

If God's first language is silence,
   why do we hear of God's Word?
If God's first language is silence,
   Does this mean words are absurd?

If God's first language is silence,
   what of the words that we pray?
If God's first language is silence
   what's the point of what we say?

If God's first language is silence,
   what of Scripture's Hebrew, Greek?
If God's first language is silence,
   are our prayers just tongue-in-cheek?

If God's first language is silence,
   in silence let us then pray.
If God's first language is silence,
   in silence commune today.

---

47. Father John was a Spanish Catholic, mystic, and Carmelite priest who was born Juan de Yepes y Alvarez. He played a major role in the Counter-Reformation in Spain and was known in Spanish as Juan de la Cruz and in Latin as Ioannes a Cruce. His poetry and publications on the development of the soul, e.g., *Dark Night of the Soul*, are considered the epitome of Spanish mystical literature.

MOTHER TERESA,[48] 1910-1997, ALBERT SCHWEITZER,[49] 1875-1965

They give us hope that love survives.

61. On Being Human

Emotions, words, the tone of voice
sometimes emerge without one's choice.
A human being's mystery
is filled with unique history:
the way at times we turn our head,
the unexpected love we spread.
The kindness and the apathy
we show, remain a mystery.
How fortunate a change of mind
when we have been overtly blind.
Though Hitler, Stalin both emerge
as human beings, they're a scourge.
Mother Teresa's, Schweizer's births
give hope, beyond all moons and earths,
a Christlike quality remains
and goodness flows in human veins.

48. Mary Teresa Bpjaxhiu, known as Mother Teresa of Calcutta, was an Albanian-Indian Catholic nun and founder of the Missionaries of Charity.

49. Ludwig Philipp Albert Schweitzer was born in the Alsace section of France. He was a Lutheran minister, theologian, organist, musicologist, writer, humanitarian, philosopher, and physician who challenged a secular view of Jesus as depicted in historical-critical method.

LUDWIG WITTGENSTEIN, 1889-1951

"Logic is not a body of doctrine. It is a mirror-image of the world. Logic is transcendental."

62. Logic

If you think something's rational,
  and this is your own view,
would some think you're irrational
  and think your view's untrue?

How is then rationality
  achieved, by a process?
Or simply by audacity
  to put forth your own guess?

If Wittgenstein[50] and Lessing[51] still
  were living, they'd aver
that logic can avoid much ill,
  wrong thinking can deter.

Use thesis and antithesis
  and see where both may lead.
Perhaps there is a synthesis
  that both sides will concede.

---

50. Ludwig Wittgenstein (1889–1951) was an Austrian-born British philosopher, and author.

51. Gotthold Ephraim Lessing (1729–1781) was a German philosopher, dramatist, author, and art critic.

63. MODERNISM

James Joyce and Samuel Becket shared
   modernist trends in lit'rature.
Wolfe, Lawrence, Faulkner also dared
   give modernism their signature.

New art, philosophy, and change
   in social organization,
Picasso's broad abstract art range
   were all a modern sensation.

And Schönberg's music called twelve-tone
   rejected well-known repertoire.
The classics were then left alone;
   Mozart, by no means, was the star.

"Enlightenment, be gone, be gone!"
   was Modernism's lasting cry.
From it a new age soon would dawn:
   new movements tend to live and die.

Selected Bibliography

D'Ambrosio, Marcellino. *When the Church Was Young: Voice of the Early Fathers*. Cincinnati, OH: Servant Books, 2014.

Aurelius, Marcus. *Meditations: Adapted for the Contemporary Reader*. Adapted by James Harris, N.p., 2017.

Bonner, Gerald. *St. Augustine of Hippo: Life and Controversies*. Cincinnati, OH: Servant Books, 2014.

Catherine of Siena. The Dialogue. Trans. with introduction by Suzanne Noffke. New York: Paulist, 1980.

Cicero Selected Works. Trans. by Michael Grant. New York: Penguin Books, 1971.

Daniel-Rops, Henri. *The Church of Apostles and Martyrs*. Vol 1. Providence, RI: Cluny, 2022.

Ephrem the Syrian. Trans. by Kathleen E. McVey. New York: Paulist, 1989.

Grant, Robert M. *Irenaeus of Lyons*. New York: Routledge, 1997.

Hildegard of Bingen. *Hildegard of Bingen Selected Writings*. Trans. by Mark Atherton. London: Penguin Classics, 2004.

Johnson, Paul. *Socrates, A Man for Our Times*. New York: Penguin Books, 2011.

Josephus, Flavius. *The Antiquities of the Jews: Complete and Unabridged*. Trans. by William Whiston. Blacksburg, VA: Unabridged Books, 2011.

Maximus the Confessor. *Maximus the Confessor: Selected Writings*. (Classics of Western Spirituality). Trans. and notes by George C. Berthold. New York: Paulist, 1985.

McKeon, Richard, editor. *The Basic Works of Aristotle*. New York: Modern Library, first edition, New York: Random House, 1941.

On Social Justice: St. Basil the Great (Popular Patristics). Trans. by C. Paul Schroeder with introduction and commentary. Yonkers, NY: St. Vladimir's Seminary Press, 2009.

Osborn, Erich Francis. *The Philosophy of Clement of Alexandria*. Cambridge: University Press, 2005.

Plutarch's Lives. Trans. by George Long and Aubury Steward. Ottawa: Canada: East India, 2021.

St. Athanasius. *Saint Antony of the Desert.* Trans. by J. B. McLaughlin. Charlotte, NC: Tan Books, 2014.

St. Gregory of Nyssa. *St. Gregory of Nyssa Collection.* N.p. Aeterna, 2016.

St. Gregory the Great, *St. Gregory the Great Collection: 3 Books.* N.p. Aeterna, 2016.

St. Isaac of Nineveh. *Headings on Spiritual Knowledge: The Second Part: Chapters 1–3* (Popular Patristics). Yonkers, NY: St. Vladimir's Seminary Press, 2022.

St. John Chrysostom. *Commentary on the Psalms.* Trans. with introduction by Robert Charles Hill. Brookline: MS: Holy Cross Orthodox Press, 1998.

St. Symeon the New Theologian. *On the Mystical Life: The Ethical Discourses, Vol. 3. Life, Times, and Theology.* Crestwood, NY: St. Vladimir's Seminary Press, 1997.

Tertullian, Cypria & Origen on the Lord's Prayer. Trans. & notes by Alistar Steward-Sykes. Yonkers, NY: St. Vladimir's Seminary Press, 2004.

The Collected Works of St. John of the Cross. Trans. by Kieran Kavanaugh and Otilio Rodriguez. Washington, D.C.: Institute of Carmelite Studies, 2017.

The Collected Works of St. Teresa of Avila. Vol. 2. Trans. by Kieran Kavanaugh and Otilio Rodriguez. Washington, D.C.: Institute of Carmelite Studies, 1980.

The Desert Fathers: Verba Seniorum III, VI, and VII (Ancient Christian Writers, 74). Trans. by Richard J. Goodrich. New York: Newman, 2020.

The Epistles of St. Clement of Rome and Ignatius of Antioch. Trans. and annotated by James A. Kleist. (Ancient Christian Writers, No. 1). New York: Paulist, 1946.

The Greek Plays: Sixteen Plays by Aeschylus, Sophocles, and Euripides. Trans. and edited by Mary Lefkowitz and James Romm. New York: Modern Library, 2016.

The Letters of Cyprian of Carthage. Vol. 2. Editors: J. Quasten, W. J. Burghardt, T. Ramsay. New York: Paulist, 1984.

Waterfield, Robin. *Plato of Athens: A Life in Philosophy.* Oxford: University Press, 2023.

Index of Names

Index of Names